OUR LOVE STORY

a keepsake journal to share with the one you love

Julie Day

CASTLE POINT BOOKS
NEW YORK

OUR LOVE STORY. Copyright © 2018 by St. Martin's Press.
All rights reserved.
Printed in China.
For information, address St. Martin's Press,
175 Fifth Avenue, New York, N.Y. 10010.

www.stmartins.com
www.castlepointbooks.com

The Castle Point Books trademark is owned by Castle Point Publishing, LLC.
Castle Point books are published and distributed by St. Martin's Press.

Designed by Hillary Caudle

ISBN 978-1-250-20347-2

Our books may be purchased in bulk for promotional, educational, or business
use. Please contact your local bookseller or the Macmillan Corporate and
Premium Sales Department at 1-800-221-7945, extension 5442, or by email at
MacmillanSpecialMarkets@macmillan.com.

First Edition: December 2018

10 9 8 7 6 5 4 3 2 1

CONTENTS

Introduction

YOUR LOVE STORY DESERVES TO BE WRITTEN. On the pages of this journal, you and your partner can celebrate what makes your relationship so special. From the first time you met, to milestones you've shared, to the private jokes that make you smile, you'll have the chance to document your unique journey as a couple.

Fill in the answers together or separately as a way to learn more about each other. Enjoy the lighthearted questions that trigger funny memories and consider deeply the ones that are closest to your hearts. Record the thoughts and words that brought you together, and begin to share the ones you have yet to say.

Make a keepsake of your relationship that will hold your favorite memories, your shared values, and the exciting plans you're building together.

OUR BEGINNING

HOW WE MET

The Day:

_____

The first moment we met was:

_____

_____

_____

check one:

♥ Serendipity

♥ Set up

♥ Meet-cute

♥ Right swipe

The first thing we thought about each other:

_____

_____

_____

_____

8

If this had never happened, we probably never would have crossed paths:

_____

_____

_____

_____

We were attracted to each other's:

_____

_____

_____

_____

The one who took the lead was:

_____

OUR FIRST DATE

Location of our first date:

_____

_____

The most memorable thing about it:

_____

_____

_____

The part that made us smile most:

_____

_____

_____

_____

The tastes, sounds, and smells:

....

....

The reason it felt different from other dates:

....

....

....

our first kiss:

♥ Sweet

♥ Sensual

♥ Sloppy

The reason we wanted a second date:

....

....

....

....

11

OUR FIRST PHOTO TOGETHER

(paste photo here)

A LITTLE ABOUT THIS DAY

OUR DATING FUMBLES

Awkward moments we can laugh about now:

_____

_____

_____

_____

Mortifying things a friend or family member did:

_____

_____

_____

_____

When we discovered each other's taste in _____, we were

_____ .

The funniest moment when meeting each other's family:

_____

_____

The scariest moment when meeting each other's family:

_____

_____

The family member who was rooting for us the whole time:

_____

The thing we'll never forget about our first few months together:

_____

The worst date we went on in the beginning:

_____

_____

_____

_____

_____

_____

_____

_____

The best date we went on in the beginning:

HOW WE CONNECT

Our favorite activities together are:

_____

_____

_____

_____

_____

Music we love:

_____

_____

_____

_____

_____

people would say we're:

♥ A balancing act

♥ A supreme team

♥ Oil and water

Food we love:

_____

_____

_____

_____

_____

_____

Places we love:

_____

_____

_____

_____

_____

_____

Our favorite secret joke:

_____

_____

_____

_____

Our zodiac signs:

_____

_____

Our favorite show to watch together:

_____

_____

Texts we're most likely to send during the day:

....

....

....

....

Our favorite online sites or memes to discuss and share:

....

....

Our song:

....

....

OUR FIRST HOLIDAY

The holiday:

_____

We celebrated with:

_____
_____
_____

♥ **Special and exciting**

♥ **Awkward but fun**

♥ **Complete disaster**

The most memorable moments:

_____
_____
_____
_____
_____

The funniest or most awkward moment:

_____
_____
_____

The holiday meal:

_____
_____
_____

The gifts we shared:

_____
_____
_____

OUR FIRST VACATION

We chose to go to _____ for our first getaway.

The highlights of this trip:

_____

_____

_____

_____

_____

_____

_____

The snafus of this trip:

_____

_____

_____

_____

_____

_____

_____

_____

_____

_____

*other trips
since then:*

♥ **Will never live up**

♥ **Are still just as good**

♥ **Are even better**

The best activity:

_____

_____

_____

_____

_____

_____

_____

_____

The most romantic moment was definitely:

_____

_____

_____

_____

_____

_____

_____

WISH YOU WERE HERE

(paste photo here)

A LITTLE MORE ABOUT THIS TRIP

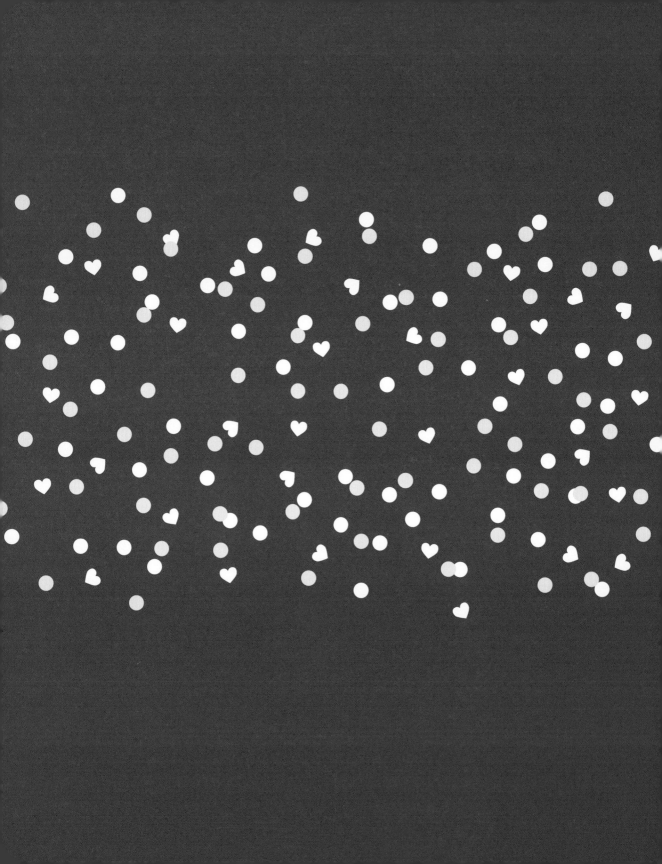

OUR ROMANCE

THE BUTTERFLIES

The special things that made us most excited about each other:

_____

_____

_____

In the beginning, we couldn't stop thinking about:

_____

_____

_____

Sparks flew when we first:

_____

_____

_____

in public, we:

♥ **Never touch each other**

♥ **Hold hands or link arms**

♥ **Go full-on PDA**

One special, loving moment that stands out to us the most:

_____

_____

_____

The first time we said "I love you":

_____

_____

_____

We still feel butterflies when:

_____

_____

_____

Three words that best describe our romance:

_____

The words or phrases we love to say to each other:

_____

_____

_____

If we could relive one day together, it would be:

_____

_____

_____

_____

_____

we feel most compatible:

♥ **In bed**

♥ **In conversation**

♥ **In both scenarios**

We have the most physical chemistry when:

_____

_____

_____

_____

_____

The little gestures that make us feel the most connected:

_____

_____

_____

_____

_____

_____

OUR DATES

Our idea of the perfect date:

_____

_____

_____

The best Sunday Funday together would include:

_____

_____

_____

The worst date we've ever had:

_____

_____

_____

we would rather:

♥ **Stare into each other's eyes**

♥ **Make each other laugh**

♥ **Hold each other**

The funniest thing that's ever happened when we've gone out together:

If we went on a double date, we'd do this:

We could skip date night altogether and do this instead:

Our dream date, if money and time were unlimited:

SPECIAL REMINDERS

Sometimes we forget to reconnect. We feel the most distant when:

_____

_____

_____

_____

It would help if _____ didn't take us away from one another so much.

When we're feeling adrift, this brings us back to shore:

_____

_____

_____

_____

_____

The best way to reconnect with each other:

_____

_____

_____

small efforts that help:

♥ **Flowers or chocolate**

♥ **A special dinner**

♥ **Getting the oil changed**

Reserving time for this activity makes us the happiest:

_____

_____

_____

Our love feels renewed when:

_____

_____

HOW WE LOVE

We show our love best by:

_____

_____

romantic gestures to us are:

♥ **An everyday must**

♥ **A special occasion**

♥ **Not that important**

We feel most loved when:

_____

_____

The secret to any loving relationship:

_____

_____

On a scale of 1-10, the importance of keeping romance alive is a: _____

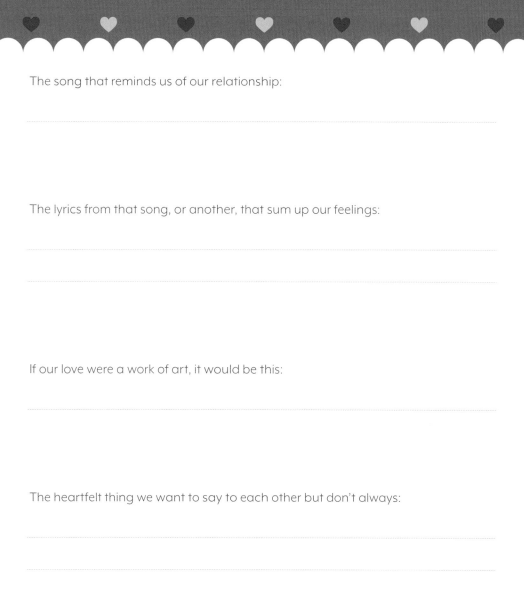

The song that reminds us of our relationship:

....

The lyrics from that song, or another, that sum up our feelings:

....

....

If our love were a work of art, it would be this:

....

The heartfelt thing we want to say to each other but don't always:

....

....

We laugh with each other most when:

_____

_____

The best product of our love:

_____

_____

We lift each other up when we:

_____

The couple who is the model for our relationship:

_____

if we were a fictional couple, we'd be:

♥ **Jack & Rose**

♥ **Hermione & Ron**

♥ **Lucy & Ricky**

♥ **Cinderella & Prince Charming**

The world falls away when we:

Our truest wishes for each other:

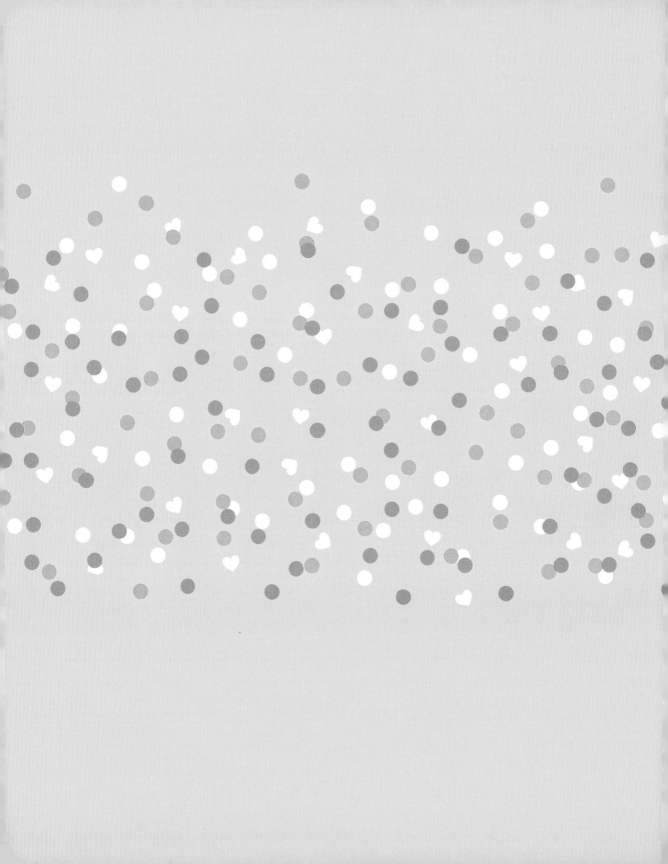

OUR FRIENDSHIP

FOUNDATIONS

This is how our friendship grew the most:

_____

_____

_____

_____

The first time we knew we had each other's backs:

_____

_____

_____

_____

_____

_____

we are best friends:

♥ **Always**

♥ **Sometimes**

♥ **We have other people for that**

We are the most alike in this way:

_____

_____

_____

We are the most different this way:

_____

_____

_____

If we were a music duo, we'd be:

_____

Things that make us cry:

_____
_____

Things that make us laugh:

_____
_____

We know we can count on each other the most when:

_____
_____

If our friendship were a house, it would be made of:

_____

Our favorite activity that no one else understands:

_____

We feel most comfortable confiding in one another when:

_____

_____

We worry what the other will think when:

_____

_____

The nicknames we use to make each other laugh:

_____

_____

Our favorite inside joke(s):

_____

The game, activity, or sport that we love the most:

_____

OUR FUNNIEST PHOTO TOGETHER

(paste photo here)

A LITTLE ABOUT THIS MOMENT:

OUR FAVORITE PASTIMES

Our all-time favorite bonding activity:

_____

If we were to do an extreme sport together, we'd:

_____

nature we love:

♥ **Beaches**

♥ **Mountains**

♥ **Deserts**

♥ **Forests**

We are bleeding-heart fans of this (or these) teams:

_____

_____

The shows we binge:

_____

_____

Our favorite meal to share:

_____

The guilty pleasure we both love and would never share with others:

_____

Fun things we introduced each other to:

_____

_____

_____

_____

_____

_____

OUR CLOSENESS

Until we met, we could never talk about this with other friends:

....

....

....

The way we show support:

....

....

....

Ways we know our friendship is special:

....

....

....

we are best at:

♡ **Listening**

♡ **Comforting**

♡ **Fixing**

Our friendship is based on these five characteristics:

....

....

....

....

We find these qualities to be the most stimulating in one another:

....

....

When we gossip, we usually talk about:

....

....

When we are stressed, we know this simple thing can calm us down:

_____

The thing about our friendship that makes us smile the most:

_____

_____

We let each other win when:

_____

_____

We feel like the same person when:

_____

we are:

♡ **Peas in a pod**

♡ **Peanut butter & jelly**

♡ **Vodka & soda**

The quirkiest things we know about each other that no one else does:

Times when we truly need each other on our team:

Times when we like each other the most:

We feel like we're telepathic when:

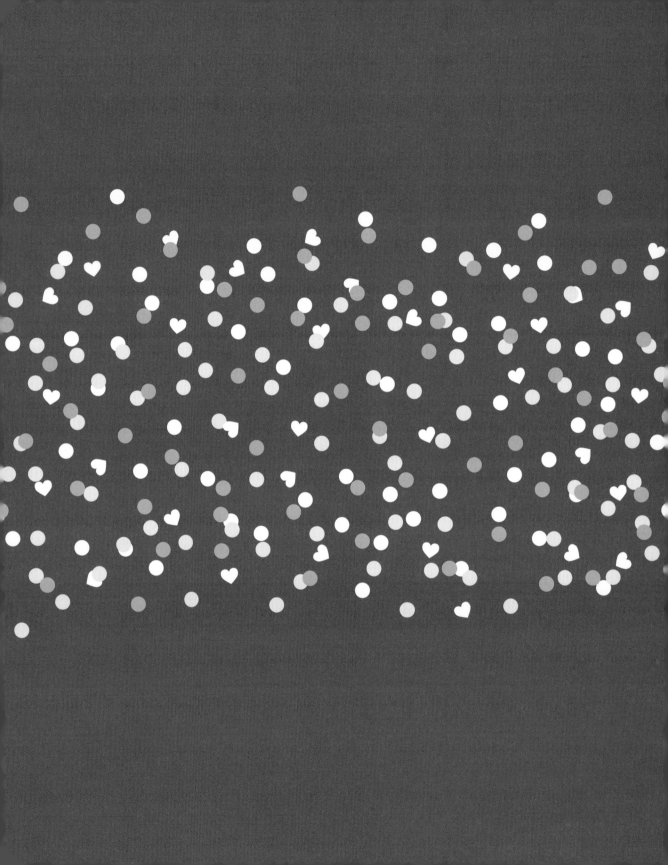

OUR FAVORITE THINGS

OUR ACTIVITIES

Our days would not feel complete if we skipped this ritual:

....

....

We cherish this special activity together:

....

....

If we sang karaoke together, this would be our go-to song:

....

If we were in an escape room, our best strengths would be:

....

we'd win any:

♥ Sack race

♥ Board game

♥ Drinking game

The sport or activity that we play best together:

_____

We are each other's MVP when:

_____

_____

Our most valued pastime as a couple:

_____

_____

Activities or sports we love but would never do together:

_____

Things we love to do with other couples:

_____

_____

OUR QUIRKS

The things that drive us nuts but we love anyway:

_____

_____

_____

Little imperfections that make each other unique:

_____

_____

_____

Our weird food habits:

_____

_____

_____

We may not have a stamp collection, but we do have:

_____

Unique places we like to visit:

_____

_____

_____

Our favorite item of clothing:

_____

The grossest food we like to eat:

_____

We would never be caught dead:

_____

Something our friends give us a hard time about:

_____

A weird trait one of us accidentally picked up from the other:

_____

_____

Our unique talents:

_____

Inanimate objects that we call by name:

_____

_____

_____

our favorite duos:

♥ **Superman & Lois Lane**

♥ **Princess Leia & Han Solo**

♥ **Homer & Marge**

Our best Halloween costume as a couple:

_____

Things we can't live without:

_____

_____

Superlatives we'd give each other:

_____

If we had alter egos, they'd be:

_____

_____

Things we made up together:

_____

_____

OUR BEST COSTUME

(paste photo here)

A LITTLE ABOUT THIS EVENT

MEMORIES WE'VE COLLECTED

Our greatest achievement together:

_____

_____

_____

Our greatest happiness together:

_____

_____

_____

Our best day:

_____

_____

_____

The biggest learning experience we've had together:

_____

_____

_____

One rainy afternoon, we:

_____

_____

_____

One sunny afternoon, we:

_____

_____

_____

A special moment with friends we adore:

....

....

Our high-five moments:

....

....

The best concert we attended:

....

Our favorite messy moment:

....

The local hangout where they know us by name:

....

If we could piece together a day of our best memories, it would be:

....

....

....

....

....

....

....

....

....

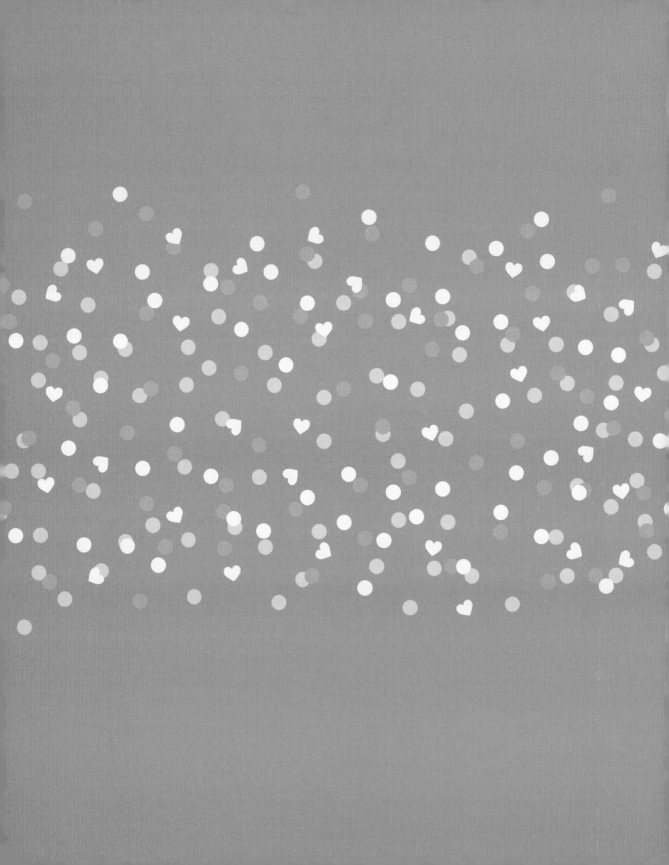

OUR VALUES

THE FUNDAMENTALS

Beliefs we share:

_____

_____

_____

The values that brought us together:

_____

_____

_____

The values that keep us together now:

_____

_____

_____

our values are:

♥ A pendulum

♥ Firm

♥ Malleable

Three important tenets of our relationship:

♥ _____

♥ _____

♥ _____

Our values were most influenced by:

_____

From the beginning, we've felt differently about:

_____

From the beginning, we've agreed on:

_____

Our deal-breakers:

_____

The things we thought were deal-breakers, but we found compromise:

_____

Our politics are similar in this way:

_____

Our politics are different in this way:

_____

The ways we work through disagreements:

_____

_____

_____

_____

How we saw things in a new light when we discussed them:

_____

_____

_____

If we were to teach the next generation one thing, it would be:

_____

_____

_____

Our values have evolved in this way throughout our relationship:

_____

_____

_____

_____

_____

_____

_____

WHEN WE SHINE

(paste photo here)

A LITTLE ABOUT THIS MOMENT

THE SMALL STUFF

We are die-hard fans of:

_____

_____

We are on the opposite team when it comes to:

_____

We would dress up in support of:

_____

We are sore losers when:

_____

_____

We'd be willing to cheat at this game:

....

This kind of music is most important to us:

....

The funniest tricks we've ever played on each other:

....

....

The comfort food we love most and can't live without:

....

....

We would sell our souls just to:

_____

_____

_____

Our silliest bad habits:

_____

_____

_____

Good habits we try to establish:

_____

_____

_____

_____

_____

_____

_____

FAMILY VALUES

Our families support us in this way:

_____

_____

_____

_____

our special days:

♥ **Days of observance**

♥ **Milestones & anniversaries**

♥ **Days that end in Y**

The rock of our family is:

_____

This ritual or observance that we cherish the most:

_____

_____

_____

_____

Our most-loved traditions:

_____

_____

The values we want to instill in our own family:

_____

_____

_____

If we were to do one thing with our family every week, it would be:

_____

_____

At our core, this is what we care about as a couple:

_____

_____

_____

_____

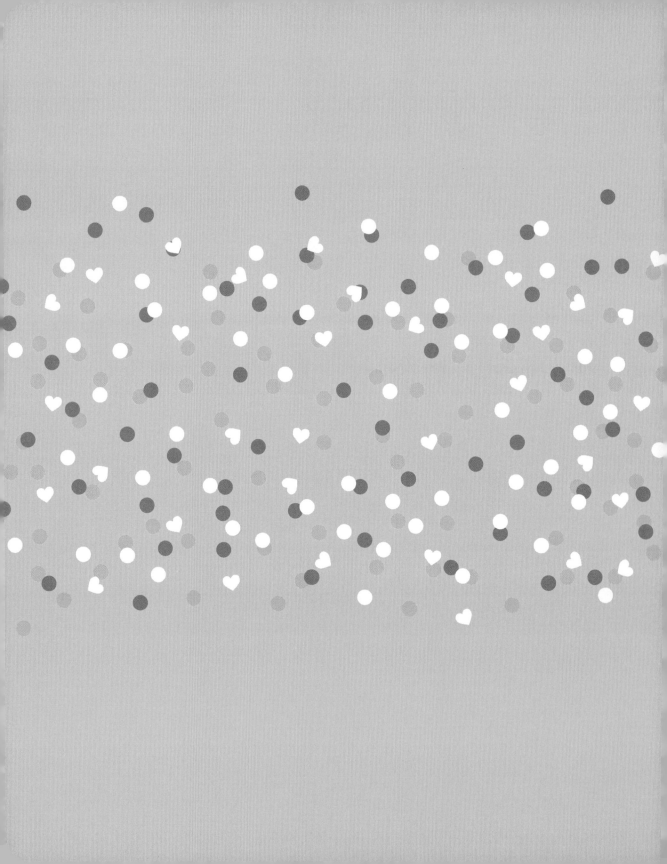

OUR FUTURE

TOMORROW AND THE NEXT DAY

Every day is a chance for us to:

_____

_____

_____

Waking up next to each other is:

_____

_____

_____

When we wake up tomorrow, this is what we should do:

_____

_____

_____

Let's spend more time together in this way:

_____

_____

_____

Something we'd like to make a habit from now on:

_____

_____

_____

Daily gestures that keep us going strong:

_____

_____

_____

YEARS FROM NOW

Five things we'd like to do together in the next five years:

- ♥ _____
- ♥ _____
- ♥ _____
- ♥ _____
- ♥ _____

Several years from now, this is where we'll be:

_____

_____

The things we look forward to further down our path:

_____

_____

This is how we'll get out of our comfort zones:

_____

_____

_____

_____

Fun things we've been meaning to do, and will set a date for:

_____

_____

_____

_____

_____

_____

reminders to our
future selves:

♥ _____

♥ _____

♥ _____

A new ritual we'd like to create to show
each other we care:

We share these inspirations for the future:

Places we'd like to travel:

Things we'd like to see:

_____

_____

_____

People we'd like to spend our time with:

_____

_____

_____

One long weekend in the future, we'll:

_____

_____

_____

On our next vacation:

If the future were a song, this is the song it'd be:

The quote that makes us most excited for the future:

In several years, this is how we'll still show our love:

Memories we'd like to make:

_____

_____

_____

When we're old and gray:

_____

_____

_____

If our present selves could remind our future selves of something,
this is what it would be:

_____

_____

US TODAY

(paste photo here)